TULSA CITY-COUNTY LIBRARY

SO-AHA-077

ceya

EXPLORING
THEATER

Music in Theater

Don Rauf

Cavendish
Square

New York

Published in 2017 by Cavendish Square Publishing, LLC
243 5th Avenue, Suite 136, New York, NY 10016

Copyright © 2017 by Cavendish Square Publishing, LLC

First Edition

No part of this publication may be reproduced, stored in a retrieval system, or transmitted in any
form or by any means—electronic, mechanical, photocopying, recording, or otherwise—without
the prior permission of the copyright owner. Request for permission should be addressed to
Permissions, Cavendish Square Publishing, 243 5th Avenue,
Suite 136, New York, NY 10016. Tel (877) 980-4450; fax (877) 980-4454.

Website: cavendishsq.com

This publication represents the opinions and views of the author based on his or her personal
experience, knowledge, and research. The information in this book serves as a general guide only.
The author and publisher have used their best efforts in preparing this book and disclaim liability
rising directly or indirectly from the use and application of this book.

CPSIA Compliance Information: Batch #CW17CSQ

All websites were available and accurate when this book was sent to press.

Cataloging-in-Publication Data

Names: Rauf, Don.
Title: Music in theater / Don Rauf.
Description: New York : Cavendish Square, 2017. | Series: Exploring theater | Includes index.
Identifiers: ISBN 9781502622716 (library bound) | ISBN 9781502622723 (ebook)
Subjects: LCSH: Musicals--History and criticism--Juvenile literature. | Musicals--Juvenile
literature.
Classification: LCC ML2054.R285 2017 | DDC 792.609--dc23

Editorial Director: David McNamara
Editor: Fletcher Doyle
Copy Editor: Nathan Heidelberger
Associate Art Director: Amy Greenan
Designer: Joseph Macri
Production Coordinator: Karol Szymczuk

The photographs in this book are used by permission and through the courtesy of: Cover
Miles Willis/Getty Images; p. 5 ilgan Sports/Multi-Bits via Getty Images; p. 7 Igor Bulgarin/
Shutterstock.com; p. 10 Hemera Technologies/AbleStock.com/Thinkstock.com; p. 12 Topical
Press Agency/Getty Images; p. 14 Monkey Business Images/Shutterstock.com; p. 18 TORSTEN
BLACKWOOD/AFP/Getty Images; p. 21 Monkey Business Images/Shutterstock.com; p. 24
KEENPRESS/Photonica World/Getty Images; p. 25 Lisa Maree Williams/Getty Images; p. 27
AP Photo/Richard Drew; p. 30 Brendon Thorne/Getty Images; p. 33 Walter McBride/Getty
Images; p. 35 In Pictures Ltd./Corbis via Getty Images; p. 38-39 Qilai Shen/Bloomberg via Getty
Images; p. 43 Dougal Waters/DigitalVision/Getty Images; p. 45 Bruce Glikas/FilmMagic; p. 48
Dougal Waters/DigitalVision/Getty Images; p. 51 In Pictures Ltd./Corbis via Getty Images; p. 53
CREATISTA/iStock/Thinkstock.com; p. 55 Mike Coppola/Getty Images; p. 58 Samir Hussein/
Redferns via Getty Images; p. 62 Bruce Glikas/FilmMagic; p. 65 Lynn Goldsmith/Corbis/VCG via
Getty Images; p. 67 Lucian Coman/Shutterstock.com; p. 69 CREATISTA/iStock/Thinkstock.com;
p. 72 Hill Street Studios/Blend Images/Getty Images; p. 79 Neilson Barnard/WireImage; p. 80 Hill
Street Studios/Blend Images/Getty Images; p. 84 danr13/iStock/Thinkstock.com; p. 87 Evgeny
Drablenkov/Shutterstock.com.

Printed in the United States of America

CONTENTS

The musical experience of *Les Miserables* can pack a powerful emotional punch.

CHAPTER ONE

BRINGING THE STAGE ALIVE

During act 1 of the musical *Les Misérables*, students band together to launch a rebellion in 1832 against the government in France after the death of General Lamarque, the only government leader who had shown empathy for the poor. The song "Do You Hear the People Sing" starts softly and steadily builds to highlight the growing strength, passion, and emotion of the students. The players sing, "When the beating of your heart echoes the beating of the drums, there is a life about to start when tomorrow comes." The idea that revolution can start as a small group of students coming together becomes even more powerful as the music climaxes and voices sing out about a willingness to fight and die for freedom.

The song shows how music can bring a theatrical production alive and captures why musicals still pack the theaters on Broadway and can have incredibly long runs. *The Phantom of the Opera* opened on the Broadway stage in 1988 and was still going as of the summer of 2016. While plays can stir emotions, musicals can heighten those feelings. They can get people singing along. The addition of music and dance to a theatrical production can make it more of a spectacle. Even in productions that are not musicals, music can be used to accentuate moods and feelings in a play.

Bringing a musical or a play with music to the stage requires many different talents. The main roles for presenting the music are held by the music director, the orchestra leader, the singers, and the musicians. A person with the technical know-how to record and play back music may be key to a production as well. Those directly involved with the music also depend on members of the crew to make the entire theatrical production come alive, such as stage managers, set designers, light technicians, and set builders.

The Building Blocks

Those directly involved in the music for a theater production have a strong background in music and music appreciation. Learning music is like learning a second language. You have to understand how to read the notes and then recreate the sounds as written. Music professionals know how music depends on timing, **harmonies**, and rhythm. And as with learning a language, mastering music doesn't happen overnight. For most who want to get involved in the musical aspect of theater, training starts young.

There's an old joke about music success: How do you get to Carnegie Hall? The answer is "Practice, practice, practice." Those who do well in the world of music know that it takes consistent dedication—

Succeeding in musical theater requires a strong background in music and performance.

repeatedly playing an instrument or singing a part. Malcolm Gladwell, the author of *Outliers*, believes in the principle that ten thousand hours of "deliberate practice" are needed to become world-class in any field. It can be boring because of the repetition required, but the payoff comes when you're able to learn something new and play it perfectly.

While many students can get musical training through school programs, some polish their skills with private lessons. Alice Meyer of Hoboken, New Jersey, has a passion for singing in musical theater. Between grade school and the age of seventeen, she performed in twenty-seven musicals, including *The Light in the Piazza, Grease,* and *Mary Poppins,* in which she played the lead. In addition to taking singing and music classes in school, Meyer has continuously trained with regular private lessons in acting, voice, and dance. She takes lessons in both ballet and in tap and jazz.

Through all the classes, she has developed technique, learned different styles, and built strength. The fact is, most roles in theater require physical stamina because they require long hours and lots of activity. You will also need stamina to sing while dancing so you don't get winded in the middle of your song. It's impossible to sing if you are out of breath. So staying physically fit is important for all cast and crew.

There is one large advantage for students in taking part in a musical rather than in a drama: there are many more roles available. You might like to sing but may not have a strong enough voice to be a lead, and you may not want the pressure of having more than a few lines. A spot in the chorus allows you to take part fully in the show and to reap all the benefits of participating. You will need to be able to learn and sing your parts, blending your voice with the others, and maybe to do some dancing. One key ingredient for a chorus member is to remain attentive during rehearsals even when you are not directly involved in the action as you will have a lot more downtime than the leads.

There is also a place for a person without a singing voice. Dancing is an important element of musical theater. Most musicals have dance numbers that will require people with those skills. If you ever took dance lessons, or even trained as a gymnast or in a sport where footwork is crucial, you can contribute to a musical. However, dancing does require coordination as well as stamina. It is not necessary for a high school student to have had formal dance training to perform in a chorus or in a lead role.

Meyer's vocal lessons show all the detail that can go into training. Her teacher puts her through many different vocal exercises, like lip **trills**, which relax the lips and warm up the voice. Other training focuses on breathing and how to use the **diaphragm** to provide breath support. Through vocal coaching, Meyer has learned to strain less and develop a stronger voice.

"I don't lose my voice because of these lessons," Meyer said in an interview for this book. "My vocal teacher has taught me how to not push too hard. When I was auditioning for *Grease*, I went to my vocal coach to review my performance of the song 'Hopelessly Devoted.' I was definitely straining and it was hurting my voice. He gave me advice on how to improve."

She learned to correct her posture and head alignment. She focused more attention on the front of her mouth and breathing correctly. She also did a ton of exercises to make her physically less tense, which made her singing less tense. In the end, she won a lead role in the musical.

For musicians, much of the same advice applies. They have to learn breathing techniques, and just as singers must learn how to listen and produce notes that are neither sharp (a little too high) nor flat (a little too low), musicians must do the same. This requires a complete mastery of their instruments. A violin player must practice to build finger strength

Musicians put in long hours of practice, learning to read music and play their instruments.

to hold down the strings in the right positions to produce the correct sounds. The trombone player must not only learn the positions of the slide, but also how to breathe and build his or her **embouchure**. The embouchure is the shape the lips must make on the mouthpiece of a brass or woodwind instrument to play it correctly.

The players build their ability to memorize as well. While the musician needs to know how to read the music and perform it, the onstage performers cannot have sheet music or scripts in front of them—they must commit it all to memory.

Anyone getting involved in musical theater might want to take drama classes or join a drama club. These classes can expose you to a variety of roles in theater and teach you specifics on what it takes to mount a powerful show. Plus, a class can provide experience and teach you skills that you can put on a résumé and that will help open doors if you want to get involved in a professional production. A student may explore a theater camp as well to make the most of summer time off.

Leadership Roles

Usually, the music director and orchestra leader work together to create the overall vision for the production and guide all cast and crew involved. Depending on how elaborate the production is, there may be a dramatic director as well as a music director. For many high school and community musical productions, one person will wear both of these hats. The director oversees the script, actors,

A Brief History of Music in Theater

For hundreds of years, plays have used incidental music to add atmosphere and mood to a production. Incidental music dates back to ancient Greece and Rome. In the fifth and sixth centuries BCE, choruses were chanted and danced between the spoken parts of Greek tragedies and comedies.

The use of music to enhance theatrical works goes back to ancient Greece.

Incidental music is usually not memorable, but there are some notable examples: Ludwig van Beethoven's music for J. W. von Goethe's *Egmont*, Felix Mendelssohn's music for William Shakespeare's *A Midsummer Night's Dream*, Georges Bizet's suites for Alphonse Daudet's play *L'Arlésienne*, and Edvard Grieg's incidental music for Henrik Ibsen's *Peer Gynt*. Shakespeare often listed music that should be played to signal the entrance of a character or perhaps enliven a battle scene.

The first theatrical piece to bring together all the elements of today's modern musical is often considered to be *The Black Crook*, which opened in New York City in September of 1866. This work used song to tell a story, along with spoken dialogue. In time, musicals developed in all different styles, from comedies to tragedies. Musicals evolved from vaudeville, burlesque, and operas. Operas certainly told a story, but they were entirely sung. The musical incorporated song along with the dramatic spoken storyline. The songs are often a continuation of the dialogue. Through the 1900s, musicals flourished and became more sophisticated. Some popular musicals are *No, No Nanette*; *Holiday Inn*; *My Fair Lady*; *Gypsy*; *The Music Man*; *West Side Story*; *Cabaret*; *Oklahoma!*; *Hair*; *Pippin*; *Phantom of the Opera*; *Les Misérables*; and *The Lion King*. *Hamilton* is a great modern-day musical that has made a huge cultural impact.

set, costuming, lighting, and sound. Typically, a music director's job involves all the musical aspects of a show—from conducting the show to deciding on musical arrangements. The orchestra leader may oversee the vocal performances as well, although this role can go to a dedicated voice or choir teacher.

Most who have these leadership roles not only have years of training in performing, they have had experience in organizing theatrical productions. They ultimately decide on the casting, the scheduling,

Choosing musicians for the orchestra is a vital part of producing a show.

and the overall vision for the production. They are often teaching everyone involved what it takes to put on a production as well as the language of theater: What does "stage left" mean, or what is "**upstage**"? Knowing the language of theater can help the team operate cohesively.

Directors at high schools, colleges, and community theaters typically have their own long history of working on musical productions during their high school and college years. Some are able to get experience at summer camps, through children's theater programs, or with church groups. Many have a master's degree and a doctorate in musical programs such as conducting, music theory, music composition, or in a specific instrument. A school music director requires at least a bachelor's degree in a music-related field and a state-issued teaching credential, according to the Bureau of Labor Statistics.

Shawn M. Riley, director of theater at Ballard High School in Seattle, Washington, for example, received a master of fine arts in directing and acting from the University of Portland. He has won multiple acting awards and gained extensive experience working in musical theater, which he brought to his job working with his high school theater programs. He dedicated years and years to honing his craft. He built a reputation for staging professional-level musicals, including *Les Misérables*, *Little Women: The Musical*, *Cabaret*, and *Bat Boy*. He said in an interview for this book that his students have been so professional, "I don't do high school theatre. I do theatre with high school students!"

Because the director works closely with a conductor, experience playing in a band or in an orchestra can help. Even without this experience, he or she needs to know how an orchestra operates and the challenges involved with preparing musicians for a performance. Directors and orchestra leaders need to keep up with the latest advances related to their field. Today's music directors can benefit from using a computer as well. For example, Finale is the worldwide industry standard in music notation software. Composers, arrangers, and songwriters use this software to create sheet music, including the score for an entire ensemble.

Interpreting the Material

A successful theatrical production with music needs players and musicians who are well trained, but when the material is performed live, it needs to be done with passion and with a point of view. This is where the music director and orchestra leader play strong roles.

They have studied scripts and how to interpret the music and words. The director will spend a lot of time getting the actors to convey their characters convincingly and to sing their parts appropriately.

"I will often direct students by asking, 'What is your intention? What is the character's motivation? Why is the character singing this song? What are these lyrics saying? What do they mean?'" said theater director Shawn Riley. "I don't want to work with robots. I want the players to have living, breathing thoughts and find out how *they* would act as the character."

Directors discuss the meanings of the artistic works with the cast and crew and may present notes on this in the program so the audiences have a full appreciation of the work they are seeing. For example, the musical *Cabaret* is a reflection on the rise of Nazism in pre–World War II Germany, and the musical *Urinetown* is both a spoof on musicals and a dystopian farce, presenting a world in which everyone must pay to urinate. A dystopian society is dehumanizing or frightening.

"That's the stuff that I love as a director—getting into the meat of any story and really talking about it," Riley said.

A musical production such as *Wicked* requires a large team of people working together.

CHAPTER TWO

THE POWER OF TEAMWORK

Above all else, theater productions depend on teamwork. In a work with music, this typically means that the core of the team will consist of the singing and dancing performers, the musicians, the orchestra leader, the choreographer, and the director. But those behind the scenes must coordinate with these people as well. Singers might take a cue to leave the stage as a lighting tech dims the lighting. The orchestra knows to begin a song after the sound technician makes the sound of thunder. The stagehand knows to drop the curtain after the major song in act 2 has ended. Everyone on a theatrical production must be in sync.

Theater teaches all involved how to cooperate. There is no room for anyone to take a star attitude or act like a diva. People who put on a play are all in it together. It's all about the "we"—what do "we" have to accomplish to make this work. Team spirit is at the core of every successful production. The individual must sacrifice for the greater whole. Theater workers are often selfless, chipping in where and when chipping in is needed. And the team members have mutual respect for each other. They understand why each role is vital. No one role is more important than another. Each member of the cast and crew has to execute his or her part perfectly because there are no second chances in live theater. Once the show is going, there is no backing up and starting again.

Being able to be an effective team player and understand the power of teamwork translates to any career. DougsGuides.com, a website dedicated to "everything you need to make the transition from college to the real world," features an article "Everything I Needed to Know About Teamwork, I Learned in High School Theatre." The title says it all.

Creating the Ensemble

With a musical theater production, there are teams within teams. The director is working closely with the singers on their dramatic performance. A choir or singing director may also come in to work specifically on how they are singing. The orchestra leader will put together a team of musicians, and they will rehearse the music. Yet another group are the people behind the scenes under the eyes of the stage manager—those who handle the lighting, sound, moving the props, and making the sets.

During the early stages of production, the teams may be working separately. As the actors bond and get closer, rehearsing their lines with the director, the musicians are off with the music director, getting their parts together. At the same time, set designers are constructing the sets, prop masters are gathering props, and lighting designers are deciding on how they will illuminate each scene.

Liam O'Bannon played tenor saxophone in the musical theater orchestra at his school in Seattle. He said as a seventeen-year-old that along with the camaraderie that develops with all the musical theater cast and crew, there is some friendly rivalry, too.

The orchestra members must rehearse their parts while the actors are learning their lines.

"Some of us in the orchestra get a little jealous of the singers because they get all the applause and attention while we musicians are in the background," O'Bannon said. "Without the musicians there would be no musical! Still, we all love the excitement of putting on a show."

In the planning stage, the music director will review the script with the rest of the creative team. He or she may share opinions on the overall concept for the musical—how the production will look on stage or how different segments may be changed. The musical director can chime in with opinions on scenery, costumes, and lighting. In some productions, a separate choreographer will be brought in to direct and plan the dance moves for the performers. The music director has to work closely with the choreographer so singing and dancing can come together seamlessly. There may be separate auditions for dancers, and this group may not interact with the others until it's time to rehearse whole scenes.

In most cases, the music director will assemble the musicians. Auditions may be required, or musicians may be selected solely on their history of performance. Sometimes a production may simply require a piano accompaniment. In other cases, only prerecorded music may be used.

When it comes time to cast the actors, the director is on hand and may work with a casting director and singing director to help choose the players with the voices best suited to each role. In high schools, music teachers may select the play based on the known talent at hand. Actors have to fit the personalities of the characters in the play and have singing voices suited to the roles.

Music and Acting Come Together

A musical requires that the actors and the musicians are closely coordinated. The musicians cannot just simply play a song. Sometimes a solo from a singer will require the band to play softly. When the entire chorus is singing loudly, the musicians should push to their full volume. In other incidences, the music will be incidental but still needs to mesh perfectly with the activity on stage. The conductor will be following the action carefully and instructing his or her players accordingly.

The coordination between singers and musicians intensifies as the opening date draws closer. Two to three weeks prior to the first live performance, the actors will go through the show as the musicians play along. Then, the real timing of scenes is established. Musicians will often have to **vamp**. Vamping is repeating a musical segment until the next actor comes on stage or completes a motion, or the audience stops clapping. In theater, professionals will often use the term "vamp until ready" or "vamp until cue." This requires that musicians play while closely following the director.

"In musical theater, there's always a vamp built in so an actor can take it as quickly or as slowly as he or she wants," said Riley, the theater director. "It drives the musicians crazy. So we try to solidify that. For example, it could be a three-time vamp or a seven-time vamp, depending on how long it takes an actor to come down a staircase."

The Team Grows Bigger

Once the actors and musicians come aboard and rehearsals begin, the team expands. As these rehearsals progress, the music director will work more closely with the lighting and set designers to make sure the ambience and setting is just right for each scene. If the action is supposed to be taking place outside in summer on a city street, the music director may give notes to the lighting director about making the stage look like a bright summer day. The set has to replicate a city street. A song may be about enjoying a sunny day, but a shift in mood comes when a thunderstorm rolls in. Again, the music director consults on how to achieve this with the lighting director and will collaborate with the person handling sound effects to discuss how a thunderclap will be produced and coordinated to fit with the music.

The music director and light director discuss ways that the lighting can subtly change to mirror the moods conveyed in the music, and also to direct the attention of the audience to certain characters at key moments. The director shares the **blocking** notes with the lighting director. Blocking establishes the positions of actors on stage at various points, and lighting decisions are made according to the

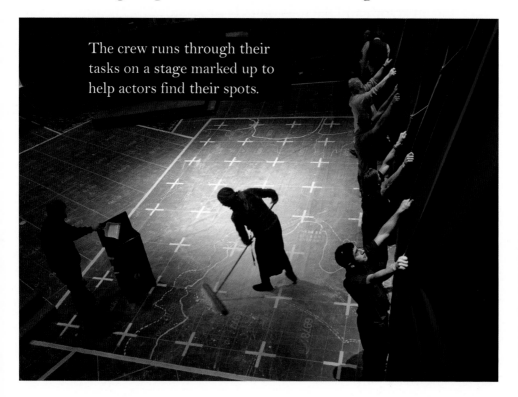

The crew runs through their tasks on a stage marked up to help actors find their spots.

blocking. In one scene, several actors are in a conversation at a party, but then one has to break from the group to perform a song that is almost like a monologue—revealing her inner thoughts. The music director and lighting director agree that the lighting on the group should go dark as the lone actor steps toward the audience, and a spotlight will follow her as she sings **downstage**.

Follow the Leader

While the group effort is essential, any show needs its leader or leaders. Ultimately, a director is calling the shots. A stage manager also is telling others what to do. Their instructions need to be followed to make things happen in a coordinated fashion. The team has to stick to the schedule that the management sets. A play usually premieres on a specific day, so all workers have to abide by a set schedule that will gradually

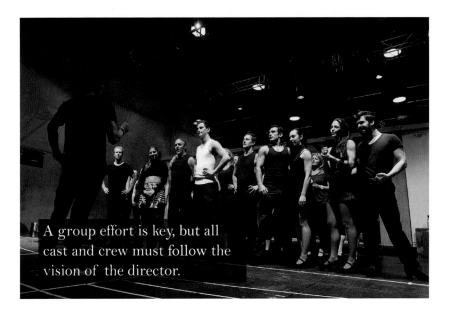

A group effort is key, but all cast and crew must follow the vision of the director.

take a production to the finish line. The scheduling of rehearsals, set design, program printing, etc., needs to be carefully plotted on the calendar. Plays are about budgeting money as well as time. Those in charge have to make sure that everyone is sticking to the schedule and the theater troupe is not spending more money than is allotted. Time management skills are not only essential for those leading operations, they are vital for all involved.

Although cast and crew must come together as a well-oiled machine, each participant must be able to work independently as well. A prop master may need to scour thrift shops on his or her own to find the perfect telephone, lamp, etc., to set the stage. A singer with a speaking part will have to go off alone to memorize lines. A musician must practice alone to learn his part as well as an actor knows his or her lines.

In high school and community theaters, everyone involved in a production comes together at the beginning so everyone can get to know each other. Each person has to know who does what. While the entire production staff is a team, there are subsets— or teams within the larger team.

Tales of Collaboration

In the summers of 2013 to 2015, a musical theater group in Portland, Oregon, showed the true meaning of teamwork in staging its original production called *J.A.W.Z. the Musical in 3D*. (After all, what could be more 3D than a live performance!) The musical was a broad spoof on the Steven Spielberg blockbuster movie Jaws. In this production, there

Award-winning Greg Kotis loves the collaborative spirit of musical theater.

wasn't just one music director but rather seven lead musicians who brought their ideas to the table. The different lead musicians collaborated on the score, bringing in music that they appreciated and wanted to put forward. The production was an example of how a small community theater can have local success. While following overall direction from two of the musicians, they met once a week for six months and gradually formed a one-of-a-kind, crowd-pleasing show. The rehearsals, costuming, props, choreography, and arranging paid off. The performances brought in full houses and raised enough money to pay for the theater rental, props, costumes, and promotion, and there was a bit left over for the performers.

Greg Kotis wrote the book and cowrote the lyrics for the musical *Urinetown*. He won a Tony Award for his book and the original score. The characters of Bobby Strong and Hope Cladwell were included on *New York Theatre Monthly*'s list of "The 100 Greatest Roles in Musical Theatre." After opening in 2001, the musical had a successful run on Broadway (965 performances), and it has lived on in many regional and school productions.

Kotis started doing theater as a sophomore in high school.

"I had no idea what to expect, but quickly learned that I loved everything about it—the people, the challenge, working together, and the rush of being in front of an audience," Kotis said.

He loves the fact that by writing original plays and musicals he can create something that feels true to his own voice and is well made. "What I write isn't always for everyone, but it's a thrill when I'm able to connect with people through my work as a playwright," Kotis said.

Kotis recommends that everyone try getting involved in a theater production because it can teach focus, courage, communication, public speaking, art history, patience, and appreciation for others. "Being part of a play or musical is a great way of exploring what you can do, how you relate to others, and you make a few friends along the way," he said.

The friends made during a production can be long lasting, and the professional connections can help if you move ahead and do more theatrical work. Actors working in a local community will often work with each other repeatedly, and the comfort of knowing each other from previous work can make the job easier. The same goes for musicians. Often the same musicians will be involved in local theater, so many form a bond that feels like family. These bonds often last a lifetime.

To stage musicals such as *The Sound of Music*, theater groups have to pay a rights fee.

CHAPTER THREE

LET'S PUT ON A SHOW

Producing any live show basically falls under three broad steps: **preproduction**, rehearsal, and staging the actual show. In a small community or high school production, the director may guide the theater troupe through all of these phases.

One of the first stages in bringing a musical to the stage is getting the rights to use the work. Publishing or licensing houses hold the rights to most plays and musicals. These organizations give legal authorization for a work to be performed, and they collect "author royalties" if the work is to be performed before an audience. A portion of the fees goes to the licensing company, and a portion goes to the creators of the stage work. Prices to license vary depending on if the theater group mounting the production is professional or amateur.

For a high school or community group, the fee can still be expensive. Rights to *The Sound of Music,* for example, cost a school $9,000. School theater director Shawn Riley describes what you get for the fee: "They send you this massive box of music—the scripts and the vocal lines—which will all have to be sent back to New York when we're done. The rehearsal package is for a twelve-week stretch—but we like to get the music in our kids' hands prior to those twelve weeks, so that's an extra $400 for every month you want the music longer."

Some of the rights might not be available if the play is being performed on Broadway or is touring, or if a motion picture based on the play/musical is in the works. Three of the biggest licensing houses are Dramatists Play Service, Samuel French, and Music Theatre International. A music director can easily comb through hundreds of musicals on the websites of these organizations. The websites present handy summaries of the plots and give quick snapshots of the number of cast members needed, the rating (like in movies—G, PG-13, R, etc.), and the number of acts. The description generally provides standard orchestration—for example, a musical might require a minimum of bass, percussion, one reed instrument, and a trombone.

When you obtain the rights, you get a conductor's score. This is sheet music that presents all the music to be played by all the instruments—the strings, the woodwinds, the brass. It can take years to master reading this, but those who take college classes on composition and music can learn this with time and experience. No matter what, you have to know what's going on with all the instruments to stage a successful production. You also get a libretto/vocal book with lyrics and spoken words, and stage directions.

After reviewing all the music, words, and lyrics, a music director might want to add a personal vision. Generally, changes, additions, and deletions require permission from the licensing house.

A score to a musical consists of sheet music detailing all musical notation for every part.

With the script and score in hand, you will know exactly how many players you will need to assemble your cast and your orchestra or band. In many professional theaters, the musicians perform in the pit, an area usually below and in front of the stage.

Casting Your Players and Musicians

An orchestra leader may choose musicians from those he or she knows personally, or may audition them. The orchestra leader has to decide who will play which parts, depending on the level of difficulty. In a high school production of the musical *Children of Eden,* there are three saxophone parts. Saxophone One is the musician who plays the leads and the more difficult solo portions, while saxophones Two and Three take on the notes to complete harmonies and triads.

The actors are typically cast via auditions. Auditions are tests in which the singers and actors come to show their skills, and the producers, director, and/or music director evaluate those trying out.

The process for attracting performers may begin with an open call for anyone to come in and audition. Community productions and bigger shows will often require headshots and résumés. Although Alice Meyer is a high school performer, she has a headshot and a résumé. She sends them in to community theater productions and her school will even use her headshot sometimes in a program or to post on display in a hallway. From headshots and résumés, a director may get a fairly clear idea of how the actors look. Some actors will simply not be physically suited for a role, so this is a good place to begin. Résumés should indicate the type of voice a performer has—baritone, soprano, mezzo-soprano, contralto, etc. Again, you can narrow down those to audition according to the types of voices suited for the roles. The résumé lists previous experience as well, which also may be weighed in the auditioning process.

Actors should become familiar with each song a character will sing during a show and should audition only for the parts that fit in their vocal range. The actors must come prepared and may sing a song that they've been rehearsing to show they are right for a

To land a role in a musical, actors present a song that shows off their vocal range.

role. They will probably be asked to read a dramatic scene as well. The right casting is critical to mounting a successful production. Directors must choose the actors who will best bring characters to life on stage. You're often looking for a unique or distinctive spirit that an actor can bring to each role. Plus, a director wants those performers who can sing on key, hit the low and high notes, and project to the back of the house. A bigger community production may use a casting agent as well. This is a professional who represents actors and can send them to audition for parts that seem suited to their singing and acting abilities and their look.

Once a director has narrowed down the possible choices for the cast, the actors will be called in for a live audition before the director, possibly the choreographer, and any prime members of the creative team, such as the orchestra leader and choir director. The audition is a daunting process for the actor. It's nerve-wracking to stand in front of a few people and give a convincing performance. The performers must come in prepared. An audition notice will state what is expected for the audition. The singers usually have to bring their own sheet music, which they will hand over to a pianist, so they can sing a favorite tune. Songs that show range, your personality, and emotional depth are usually wise choices.

As an auditioning singer, you are relying on the accompanist in the room, so be courteous, friendly, and be sure to thank them. Who knows, they may have a voice in the casting process. Many directors will let you sing just sixteen or thirty-two bars because they don't have time to go beyond that.

Kate Lumpkin, a freelance casting assistant, gives this advice on the blog stageagent.com: "The thing that impresses me the most in an audition room is when someone walks in knowing exactly who they are and honors their truths. You can tell instantly. It is very rare, but when I see it I am instantly hooked. This is clearly not something you can buy at a store. I have found that people who take the time to establish a sense of style that represents who they are have a much stronger tendency to feel comfortable in their own skin, which is the first step towards honoring your truths in the audition room. This is far more important than any heel height or suit cut."

As the director, you may give a few notes of criticism to see how the performers respond and interpret your direction. This interaction can also help a director gauge how well he or she can work with an actor. How well an actor takes direction can make an impact on whether a person gets cast or not.

If you are casting for a musical, it's very likely your actors, including chorus members, will be dancing, so the audition may require that a performer do a few easy steps that the music director and choreographer can judge. For the most part, choreographers are not always concerned about how well the steps are performed; they are more focused on an actor's energy and simple ability to move to the beat. However, if the musical demands tap dancing or ballet, an actor will have to be ready to bring on the moves. In general, however, looking like you're enjoying yourself will beat a serious look of concentration.

Let the Rehearsal Phase Begin

Once the players and musicians are cast, the rehearsal phase can start. Typically, a musical will demand a rehearsal schedule of six to eight weeks, although some schools can stage a production with four weeks of intensive rehearsals. Scripts and vocal scores should be given to cast members at least a week before the first rehearsal. Even if you're doing a community or school theater production, you might have performers sign letters of commitment so

Theater groups may have performers sign letters showing their commitment.

they know that this is a serious endeavor. The note stresses that the actor agrees to show up on time for all rehearsals, performances, and related activities. For example, student singers in musical theater productions at Ballard High School in Seattle must sign a contract agreeing to the time commitment, rules, and expectations. The contract shows that being in a high school musical is a serious matter and you have to be ready to work hard.

While actors are off studying their scripts, so is the director. As the director, you are deciding how to best approach each scene and song for the best effect. Your ideas might need to be supported by those in the crew handling lighting, sound, and scenery.

At the first rehearsal, everyone comes together from the cast and crew. Everyone involved might make an introduction to the group. This is a chance for everyone to meet so they know who is on the team. As a director, you will make some introductory remarks introducing yourself, talking about the play or musical, and telling what to expect in the months ahead.

Directors often make sure to keep a sheet with everyone's phone numbers and emails—this contact sheet can help all cast and crew with various parts of the process, from sharing rides to arranging rehearsals. Also, emergency contacts are needed as well. If anyone should have an accident or fall ill, you need to know who to call. Ask if anyone has any special health needs or requirements. Directors may want to remind their singers to stay healthy and get plenty of rest—a stellar performance depends on voices that don't sound raspy or strained, or sinuses that aren't clogged. Plus, singing and playing the music repeatedly for a show requires a lot of energy, which can be exhausting. A show depends on a healthy, well-rested cast and crew.

Sometimes in a small-production musical, actors in lesser roles will learn the parts of the leads just in case they should have an emergency and not be able to make the performance. In bigger productions, all the leads will have **understudies** (performers who learn another's role in order to be able to act as a replacement at short notice).

In April of 2016, the lead actor for Cirque du Soleil's first Broadway musical, *Paramour*, dropped out just two weeks before it was to open for previews. (Previews are performances before the show has officially opened. The creative team is still fine-tuning and making tweaks in the show during previews prior to its "official" opening. Critics have not yet reviewed the production in previews and tickets are often discounted.) The lead actor in Paramour left because of creative differences, but the show had to go on, so the production team quickly found a seasoned Broadway musical actor to replace the suddenly departed lead. In a high school production, a similar thing can happen, so it's good to have a backup plan. Often cast members familiarize themselves with other parts so in case an emergency comes up and someone drops out, someone else can fill in.

A music director may keep a list of backup musicians as well, and depending on how big the production is, there may be an understudy for each musician. If one takes ill for the night, you need to have a musician ready to jump in, read the music, and ensure the show will go on.

Getting Down to Business

Even on this first day, a music director might jump into blocking a scene, having the actors try moves onstage as they say their lines or sing their songs. As a director, you may try to position the actors in different spots as they proceed through their motions, and keep notes on the script as to what works and what doesn't. The actors should jot down notes after they practice a scene so they can study their moves later. The director must make sure that the stage manager has these notes on blocking. He or she will keep track of blocking decisions to make sure actors get into proper positions and follow agreed-upon cues during the real performance. The stage manager keeps track—getting rid of discarded notes and recording the newest decisions. An actor may keep a notebook about blocking as well.

Setting a tone of professionalism, giving your best work, and high expectations can help pave the way for quality work throughout the process. Early on, a director may have to step up and make it understood that lateness and being unprepared will not be tolerated. If one person slips up, it affects everyone else in the performance. Actors need to have done their homework and come in with lines memorized. That said, the first few weeks are ones of trial and error. Nothing is perfect at the start, and the process is about exploring and finding what does and doesn't work.

Having lines committed to memory is critical because then the director and actors can focus more on the character development and the movement on

While actors often hold scripts in first rehearsals, they soon must memorize lines.

stage. Still, it's reasonable to expect that during the first few weeks the performers will be "**on book**," meaning they will be reading from the script to some degree. A few weeks in, however, actors need to be "**off book**" for the most part, delivering all lines without the help of a script in front of them. A stage manager or assistant director may be on hand to feed lines to actors who struggle in patches.

Another player who may be in the inner circle of the creative teams is the choreographer. He or she will collaborate closely with the director, instructing the actors in any dance motions that are needed as they sing or move to the music.

Musical Directing Stars Are Born

From the age of two, Todd Ellison sensed that he would be a conductor or music director. Even at that age, his parents said he would move his hands to music as if conducting. When he saw his first Broadway show as a kid, he looked into the orchestra pit and saw a guy waving a stick and he thought that was the job for him. He began taking piano lessons at age six. Growing up in Connecticut near the Goodspeed Opera House in the town of Haddam, Ellison got a job as an usher the year after the musical *Annie* had a run there. He went on to the Boston University School of Music to get a degree in piano performance. Starting with Off-Broadway productions, he built a stellar reputation as a piano player, conductor, music supervisor, and director. He has served as music director for Broadway productions like *Annie* and Monty Python's *Spamalot*.

Luis Perez followed a different path to a career as a music theater director. He was a chemistry major and math minor in high school. His parents expected him to be a medical doctor like they were. But his life course shifted when he fell very ill in high school. He had been very athletic, participating in football, martial arts, and track. After being bedridden for weeks, he wanted to figure out a way to get back on his feet again. His girlfriend suggested taking dance classes. At age fifteen, he got totally hooked. His parents weren't thrilled but they said if he could get all As, he could study with the Joffrey Ballet in New York City. He danced professionally until age twenty-seven, when another accident changed his course again. After he suffered a hip injury, he auditioned for roles in musical theater. He landed parts in *Phantom of the Opera*, *West Side Story*, and other productions. He also served as the choreographer on several shows. With such a broad background in musical theater, Perez was able to land a job as the head of Roosevelt University's musical theater program in Chicago. Each year now, he directs and choreographs at least one musical on the University's O'Malley Theatre stage.

Todd Ellison (*right*) was bit by the musical theater bug at a young age.

You will have to carefully schedule each day and make sure you are reaching certain goals. You want to set **rehearsal calls** and assure that all parts of the production are being rehearsed in time for opening night. In a musical, all the musicians are not typically there as the actors are being rehearsed. Often it may be just the director, the actors, and a piano. The music director will play through the songs for the singers and the full instrumentation will come later. In rehearsals, the music director may first run the company through some vocal warm-up exercises before working on the actual songs. The chorus may rehearse their vocal parts in a music room, and dancers may practice in another space to recorded music.

Practice Makes Perfect

When the music director brings the musicians together for a few days of rehearsals without the singers, these rehearsals are called band calls. The director makes sure the performances and notes are all hitting the mark. Then, on another day, the cast will have a "sitzprobe," or a seated rehearsal. The cast comes in and sings along with the live music, but they do not act out their roles. Then, a production often has a "seating call," during which the musicians review exactly where they will be sitting for the performance, and microphones and other technical issues are checked.

The technical crew works closely with the musicians on this, making sure microphones are in the right place and assuring the audio equipment is properly adjusted for solo performances. With the performers, the sound technicians have to test the mic packs, which are commonly used in theatrical productions. A mic pack has a transmitter that is basically the size of a pack of playing cards and runs on batteries. Techs must make sure that the batteries are fresh and will not die, or there will be no sound in the audience. A microphone is attached somewhere near the singer's mouth. A thin wire runs from it to the transmitter pack hidden somewhere in the actor's costume. The transmitter sends an audio signal to a central receiver, which then sends the sound to speakers in the theater. It's essential for the tech crew to review that all this works right. And as singers move about, especially in dance numbers, they need to know that their mic packs are securely attached to their bodies. Costume designers have to take mic packs into consideration, too. They have to create a place for actors to strap on and hide these devices. The mics must also be free from friction with the costume as that could create unwanted noise.

As the actors move about on stage in rehearsal, props and furniture may not have been constructed yet, so a stage manager may mark off in tape where set items will be placed. The actors work around these marks until the real items are ready.

When the actors go through their scenes and songs, a music director gives them notes when they are done. Advice might be to try saying a line softer, to try turning your body suddenly when someone walks in the door, or to try saying the line as you walk to the fridge and take a soda out. This is a time to see

During rehearsals, the cast makes note of the director's changes.

what works and doesn't. The actor or singer should keep a notebook handy to keep track of notes and review them.

At the end of a full cast rehearsal, the director may give the cast notes and the crew directions. Notes can be about the naturalness of the interactions. Actors can sometimes know the words so well that they are delivering the words correctly, but they are not thinking about what they mean. The actors may not appear to be conveying emotion as they talk. Or maybe they don't seem to be listening to the other actors. Sometimes, actors will rush the lines, and they will lose impact or not be understood. Often, a director has to remind the actors to think of the meaning of what they are saying. Giving positive feedback builds a better production as well. Actors and crew will be lifted by compliments and cheerleading.

After rehearsing scenes in chunks, the music director will want to conduct a run-through, either doing the whole play top to bottom or doing an entire act straight through. This will give a sense of flow and make it easier to see what sections might need more work compared to others. When the actors can do a complete run-through, a tech rehearsal can be scheduled. This is a time when all members of the cast and the orchestra must be at full attention. In a musical, there can be a large number of people on stage at one time. There can be some confusion with lots of people coming on and off stage. Dancers and chorus members need to listen to any changes made in stage directions so they can enter and exit on time and without causing chaos.

In a tech rehearsal, the full cast and crew go through the entire performance—doing lights, props, scene changes, and sound effects. A music director may sit at different parts of the theater during rehearsals, checking the **sightlines** to see how the show will appear to all members of the audience no matter where they are seated.

A Tech Check

A tech rehearsal may be done first with the actors not in costume, but a dress rehearsal will have to be conducted as well. Actors will be in complete costume to see how they are fitting and to run through costume changes. Plus, you want to see how costumes appear under different types of light. This is also the time to make sure everything can be seen and heard. Again, after a tech rehearsal, it's crucial to give notes and address any technical problems. If things aren't working, now is time to fix them.

The lighting technicians will have lights of various strengths and colors attached to **battens** and bars in the ceiling. They will have to carefully rig the lights during the tech rehearsal to get all the needed effects. This may mean adjusting the **barn doors** on the lights to direct light beams. Electricians may have power cords plugged into **dips** on stage, and they have to make sure all electrical gear is operating well and no one will be tripping over cords.

During final tech rehearsals, all **set dressing** will be in place so the actors can perform with all the scenery and props that will be on the stage during the live show.

Final rehearsals with all elements in place including the band or orchestra must also be scheduled. Many theater directors and producers recommend taking a day off before the opening night so the cast and crew are totally rested.

All members must pay close attention during rehearsals for the **curtain call** as well. How the performers come out to take their bows needs to be coordinated and look just as professional as the rest of the show. The curtain call is not in the script, but it is certainly part of the play. It's the time when all involved receive their reward for all their hard work.

In a tech rehearsal, the lighting and sound crew members have a chance to review all cues.

Completing the Picture

Along the way, you also have to schedule your cast for costume fittings. For a small community or school ensemble, this may mean that they are bringing in clothes from home or shopping at a thrift store or costume shop on a limited budget. If the musical is a period piece—*Oklahoma* or *Brigadoon*, for example—costumes may be necessary. A costume designer or seamstress will have to spend time with the actors, getting measurements. Costumes must be ready in time for a few dress rehearsals so actors can get used to moving in them and a designer can make any adjustments in waist sizes, sleeve lengths, etc. Zippers cannot afford to get jammed, and pants need to stay up. No one wants a wardrobe malfunction while on stage. A director may keep a seamstress in the **wings** with needle and thread at the ready during all performances just in case something goes wrong with the clothing. Costumes need to be able to survive vigorous dance numbers.

Musicians generally wear their own clothes, which are usually black or dark so they cannot be easily seen and distract from the action onstage. Sometime, a production will want to add class and have musician dress in formal attire, such as tuxedos and black dresses.

Show Time Arrives

After weeks of long days and nights working toward a perfect show, the debut arrives. Opening night is a time to be nervous, and that nervous energy can lead

Makeup can be essential in creating an actor's look and character.

to a strong performance. For the director, your hard work has been done, and the efforts of your hard work will be apparent now in the work of the cast and crew. Still, your role as cheerleader continues on opening night, and you will be checking that all people and parts are in place for a smashing debut. Like a coach, you may give a quick speech praising everyone's hard work and encouraging everyone to do his or her best out there tonight. Check your watch and make sure all cast and crew are ready to go at showtime as promised.

Sound crews arrive early to check microphones, charge batteries on microphone packs, and put any mics in dressing rooms. The prop crew checks that all props are in position, carefully checking the prop list. The wardrobe team reviews all the clothing, assuring that garments are laundered and fully repaired. The lighting crew has its list of cues to follow and checks that the lights are all in working order. The sound crew reviews its notes as well. In most productions, lighting and sound crews will be able to communicate with the stage manager through light headsets. All cast members must arrive early to put on their makeup—or have it applied by a makeup artist—and to warm up. Singers need to warm up their vocal cords so they are ready for their first note. Anyone who dances will need to stretch so they can be ready for their numbers. Actors will review timing or troublesome lines.

In this production, the tab curtain that hides the wings rises and the producer comes out to say

All the hard work of rehearsal pays off in a student performance of *Peanuts*.

a couple of preliminary words. When she or he is done and leaves the stage, the music begins. As the curtain rises, the **beginners** are in place. Everyone hopes all the rehearsing and preparation pays off. The lead actors move downstage to the **apron** and deliver their opening song in the **footlights**. The first scene ends, and the stage manager stands in the prompt corner and cues the stagehands to change the set. The audience is applauding and laughing. Things appear to be going well. The female lead has to run offstage for a costume change and the second scene. It requires great speed and the help of the dresser, who will help her into a new outfit. Each act proceeds along as rehearsed and the end will result in an ovation from the audience.

Meanwhile in the Pit

The musicians arrive early as well to warm up. They need to limber up their fingers and get their lips ready. They review their music and focus their concentration on what is to come. They may play scales to make sure they have the notes right or review a tricky part. Some will review in their performance area or they may go backstage to go over what they need.

Live music is so important to a production that it may seem unfair that the musicians and music director are often out of sight, off in the wings or down in the orchestra pit. On the other hand, the audience is not looking at the musicians, so that role can be less stressful than being on stage. The musicians' spaces are often cramped and dark so they will go unnoticed during the performance. The musicians typically have lit music stands to allow them to read their sheet music. In some well-equipped theaters, they will have monitors to watch the conductor without taking their eyes off the music sheets. In many cases, the musicians cannot see the performance, but the conductor can. The conductor is the link between the actors and the musicians. The musicians may jot notes down on their score—play louder here or be ready to vamp for a long time. Sometimes they jot down notes to make sure they are coming in at the right points.

After the curtain rises, the director might play a role in keeping things quiet backstage. Squash all cell phone chatter and texting. Make sure people are where they are supposed to be. However, a stage manager might be able to handle all this, and you'll be better off in the audience, watching the production and making notes about what's going right and what needs work. Save giving any notes until the next day because opening night is always a time of celebration, and deservedly so. As the run continues, you are expected to be there at each performance to lend support. Sometimes the cast may call the music director up on stage to take a bow. At the very end of the last performance, you may be called out to make a speech summing up the whole production.

A final concern is the cast party. On opening night and closing night, there may be a celebration to recognize all the sweat, muscle, time, and brainpower that have gone into the effort. A producer should add this into the budget. Then, when the run is completely over, the theater group will have to **strike** the set, clean up, and start thinking about plans for the next production.

Even professional performers like Madonna have taken a stumble during a live show.

CHAPTER FOUR

HANDLING THE PITFALLS

L ive dramatic and musical theater by its nature has the potential for things to go wrong. In a television show or movie, the director can simply yell cut, and the action can be repeated in another take. Live performers do not have that luxury. The history of theater and musical theater is full of pitfalls. In fact, a number of performers have taken a misstep and actually fallen into the pit—the orchestra pit.

That's exactly what happened to the singer Manoel Felciano, who was an understudy for the role of Judas in *Jesus Christ Superstar*. He usually played one of the disciples, but one night the regular Judas took ill. Near the end of his first song, the highly charged "Heaven on Their Minds," Felciano made a very dramatic rush to the front of the stage and suddenly disappeared. The audience heard a body fall and the orchestra somewhat hesitantly finish the music. As the next number began, the conductor helped boost Felciano back on the stage. The audience went crazy with applause, relieved that the actor was OK. There is nothing like empathy to win an audience over.

Technical Difficulties

Gus Moody of New York City has been performing in musicals since he was a youngster. By the age of sixteen, he had done *Anything Goes, Guys and Dolls, Aladdin, Les Misérables, The 25th Annual Putnam County Spelling Bee,* and *All Shook Up.* He also served as the sound director on a production of *Peter Pan,* where he had to provide both music and sound effects. He decided on music for entrances, exits, and the beginning and end of scenes. He chose the music from royalty-free websites. He was also in charge of lighting and rehearsed a bit of singing in the production. He found it to be a job that required great coordination and one in which it was easy to make mistakes.

Moody had a script that he marked up with notes indicating when sounds needed to be played and when lighting changes needed to happen. The sound and light cues were essential to the actors. For example, when the lighting changed from red to blue, it might cue the actors to enter and start the next scene. When they heard a crash sound, that might be a cue for actors to leave the stage so a big dance number could start.

"I knew if I messed up sound or lighting, I would mess up the performers on stage as well, " said Moody in an interview for this book. "I had to tell the lighting designer throughout the show when to change the lights, while simultaneously doing all the sound. Occasionally, I got mixed up. So a light might come on too late or a few lines were delivered in very dim light. During one performance, I started playing the prerecorded finale music when it wasn't the last scene yet. I had to stop it and reset everything, and redo it."

Despite all the troubles in the school production, the show went on and it was a success—and the audience was forgiving of the mistakes.

Liam O'Bannon, who plays the tenor sax in musicals at his high school, said in an interview that multiple rehearsals make the performances almost error-free. Sometimes, however, someone in his orchestra will make a mistake and play a wrong note, but the rest of the musicians keep playing so it covers any wrong notes that might pop up.

Tech crew members on high school productions have to be on the alert to avoid and solve problems, too. A singer's mic might rub against a costume and create a distracting sound. A costume designer has to be aware of any way an outfit might interfere with a microphone. On occasion, a radio signal could be picked up by the mics—sound technicians may learn approaches to stop interference.

Even Pros Make Mistakes

Community and school productions try to make the best sets possible, but occasionally parts of sets fail and songs can be interrupted, requiring improvising when things don't function as planned. This even happens in professional productions. While performing in the musical Wicked, Idina Menzel portrayed the Wicked Witch. During her melting scene, she would fall through a trap door. In her second-to-last performance in the role, she fell too

One day after fracturing her ribs, *Wicked*'s Idina Menzel returned for a final bow.

hard through the trap door and broke a lower rib. Her understudy took over for the final performance and misfortune struck again. During one song, the understudy had to appear as if she was flying while standing on a cherry picker (a platform that can be raised or lowered at the end of a hydraulic lifting system). However, during this last show, the lifter didn't lift. What did the fast-thinking cast do? They all squatted down low to pretend as if the singer was floating far above their heads.

Stagehands have to be on the alert for any potential dangers. Even a bit of spilled water can send dancers slipping and taking their own catastrophic spill.

A video on YouTube of musical theater bloopers (https://www.youtube.com/watch?v=xGAVvbz_S1w) shows actors in a very dramatic scene in *Les Misérables* unable to stop laughing and sing their parts when something happens to one of them. She appears to have swallowed something and has difficulty regaining her poise.

Playing for Laughs

Playing a mistake for laughs is often the best approach. An audience can appreciate a mistake and laugh in sympathy along with the struggling performers.

In *Newsies*, one singer's moustache began to flop off his face. Another actor smoothly pushed it back on, but not before the audience began howling with laughter.

In a production of *Bloody, Bloody Andrew Jackson,* a lot of fake blood is spilled on the stage. One night, a lead singer made his entrance, wiped out in the blood, and took out some stage lights as well. But in the old stage tradition, he just kept on singing, and the audience didn't register anything was amiss. A dog who had a starring role in Shakespeare's Two Gentlemen of Verona took a liking to an actor's nether region. The actor went with the flow and it certainly added extra laughs to the production

The musicians in the orchestra pit often seem to be in the line of fire when it comes to mistakes. In the musical *Her First Roman,* the chorus girls would stuff clothes under their wigs to give volume and help keep them from flopping. When the lead actress saw a bra peaking out from beneath one wig one night, she **corpsed**—she started laughing uncontrollably and peed on the floor, which tilted slightly, directly into the orchestra pit. In one performance of *Les Misérables,* Andrea McArdle forgot she had colorful M&Ms in her pocket. When she tossed her body back in a powerful death scene, out came the candies, showering all the musicians in the orchestra in a rainbow of colors.

Sometimes actors will be a little playful or bored during a production and they will try to get a fellow actor to corpse. The cast members in the old *Carol Burnett Show* were famous for this. (Take a look on YouTube to find examples.)

When someone makes flubs on stage, "corpsing" can be the best solution.

High and Low Notes

The music director and orchestra can often help save the day when something goes wrong. Sometimes an actor will speak more slowly than expected or there will be some sort of delay in the action. In musicals, there is something called "round-and-round" bars, where a bar of music can be repeated over and over again as needed if something isn't quite going right on stage. For example, scenery may be stuck and the stage hands need a bit more time to set things straight. The conductor sees the problem and signals the musicians to keep playing. The audience is none the wiser. Scenery in a big musical can often be a source of headaches. Some giant sets may be automated to move using computers, and things don't always move as they should.

Musicians can make mistakes, too. In the musical *Kiss of the Spider Woman*, an understudy sat in on keyboard one night. As the music started, the conductor and cast heard an odd quavering sound from the keyboardist. It took a minute to figure out the leg of the nervous keyboard player was shaking nonstop on the volume pedal.

In an early performance of *Seussical*, the music director Seth Rudetsky freaked out halfway through the first act. Rudetsky was playing the piano and noticed the cast looking at him oddly. A giant waterbug appeared to be hovering just above his arm, about to land. For some it wouldn't have been a problem, but Rudetsky had a tremendous fear of insects. Luckily, the bug missed landing on his arm and crawled away.

Musicians and music directors also have to be careful not to overbook. Music professionals can be in high demand, so they can get many offers. But if you take on too much work, you won't be able to meet the demands of all the jobs, and your work will suffer. Ultimately, you'll build a reputation of being unreliable and not get called back.

Averting Disasters and Facing Them Full On

Sometimes, musical actors have to think quickly to avoid disaster. In a performance of the musical *1776*, the singer playing Ben Franklin stepped on Martha Jefferson's dress. The actress went off script and told old Ben, "You are standing on my dress!"

Careful planning can keep
actors on the stage from being
left in the dark.

The audience thought it was part of the show and a wardrobe disaster was averted.

In the musical *The Pajama Game*, a lead actress is supposed to catch a pencil that is thrown at her and then do some fast, complicated math on a pad. In one performance, the actress didn't catch the pencil. Left with nothing to write with, she quickly ad-libbed: "I'll do the math in my head." Thinking fast on your feet can certainly save the day when a mistake is made.

Sometimes, however, minor disasters cannot be covered up, but hopefully the audience is forgiving. At a performance of the musical *Dirty Rotten Scoundrels*, the understudy filled in for the actor/singer John Lithgow. However, in one number, he totally forgot the first forty seconds of the lyrics. He was well rehearsed, but sometimes you can just go blank on stage. The conductor tried to mouth and whisper the words to him, but he just couldn't get it. Fortunately, he finally remembered the rest of the song and the musical continued uninterrupted.

In a touring performance of Rent, the power went off in the middle of a major song. Although the microphones were shut off, the cast powered through and kept singing. For the audience, it was a special and amazing moment.

Rules of Theater Etiquette

Keeping things orderly in the theater plays a role in preventing distractions and mistakes. Orderliness begins with rules of theater etiquette. Both the audience and the cast and crew have their distinct rules to follow. Theater etiquette that applies on Broadway also applies for schools and community productions.

Students need to tell parents and friends that a general rule of thumb is to arrive at least thirty minutes before a performance, or fifteen minutes at the absolute latest. Those attending must be seated before the houselights can be turned down and the curtain can rise. Someone arriving late can throw off the onstage action. If a person does arrive late, advise them to consult with an usher who may be able

Audience members are advised to follow certain rules, such as turning off cell phones.

to sneak them in at an appropriate moment (with a guiding flashlight) so they don't disturb the show or trip in the dark. Other common advice to share with your audience: Turn off cell phones and don't talk during the performance. Don't wear a hat that will block the view for those behind you. Stay through the whole performance—leaving is considered rude. Do not take photos. Feel free to applaud and react—at the appropriate moments.

Just as with the audience, the cast and crew must be on time! Call time is the time the cast and crew is expected to be at the theater and ready to work. For cast and crew, quietness is a general rule when not performing. Everyone must make sure his or her mobile phone is off and put away. Paying attention at all times is critical, and missing a cue is unacceptable. A text on a cell phone can be a costly distraction. Always listen to the stage manager or conductor, as the case may be. They may have instructions that diverge from the rehearsed action, and these directions must be followed. Actors who step offstage, need to be out of the way with no talking and no loud noises backstage. Go to assigned areas where you can be called for your next scene.

Performers and musicians do not mingle with the audience before a show. It detracts from the special feeling of the performance. Musicians and actors should never talk when their director is talking. All staff members need to know their cues. Musicians need to know when to come in. Actors need to know when to make their entrances. Singers need to know when to start belting it out. Actors and musicians should accept all notes and criticism graciously and address them. In general, these performers should not be giving each other notes; notes should only be coming from the director or stage manager.

For actors, do not linger in the wings to watch the show—most likely you'll just be in the way and a distraction. The time to watch the show is during run-throughs before the dress rehearsal. If actors are in the wings, they are often hidden behind curtains called legs, waiting to make an entrance. If something needs to be added or removed from a costume, ask the costume designer. Keep your area neat and clean, whether it be in the orchestra pit or in the dressing room. Take care not to brush against sets or scenery—it can damage or knock things out of place so they don't operate correctly. Actors should also check their props before show time—you don't want to come up empty handed on stage. Be patient during tech and full rehearsals. There may be a glitch with something or someone, and you may be asked to wait a long stretch before forging ahead. Always give your best, and always be respectful of everyone in the theater.

Public speaking skills are among the talents developed in the theater.

CHAPTER FIVE

REAL-WORLD MUSIC MAN

Bernadette Quigley has had a long career acting in film, television, plays, and musicals. At a young age, she was cast as Maria in *West Side Story*. She was not naturally a singer but she had great determination. "I took an insane amount of voice lessons," Quigley said, "and I eventually hit the notes that Maria had to hit."

Her determination, which she developed through performing, has helped her to thrive and survive in the real world. Today, she earns a living as a part-time actress and part-time publicist.

As a publicist, she uses many of the skills she forged in theater. In theater, she continually has to accept rejection and sell herself. Getting a story in the press for a client requires the same, and Quigley knows that, as with acting, success is a numbers game. The more auditions she goes on, the more work she gets. The more pitches she makes for clients, the more press she gets for them. Plus, in theater, Quigley sharpened her delivery and became a powerful speaker. Just like she may act in a musical, she sometimes sees her role as a publicist as another role—she delivers her lines with enthusiasm and confidence and that helps get ink for her customers.

High school student Gus Moody found that being in musicals has boosted his confidence and his ability to work with others and talk to strangers. In his performance of *The 25th Annual Putnam County Spelling Bee*, he was required to pose as a parent of one of the students in the bee. The show is set up as if you're watching a spelling bee. As part of the musical, he had to be in the lobby and in the audience. He would walk up to those attending the play, point to the program and say: "That's our daughter. She's going to win. Cheer for her."

"It was highly improvisational—interacting with the audience," said Moody. "Throughout the show, I had a seat in the audience. Whenever my daughter would come on stage, I would turn to the person next to me and say, 'I'm so proud of her and she's done so great.'"

Those who work on the music side develop many of these same skills—they know how to sell themselves, handle rejection, work with others, and build up confidence in their talents.

Business Values Theater People

An article in *Dramatics* magazine featured interviews with CEOs who spoke about why they like to hire people who have been involved in theater productions.

One said, "Theatre students have done extremely well with us, and we usually hire them because they're well-disciplined workers who learn quickly and give of themselves to the company."

Another added, "We like to hire theatre students, but it is a shame that when they apply to us they don't seem to realize their strengths and advantages."

The business leaders expressed their appreciation of the "let's-get-it-done" attitude that most theater people have. Plus, theater people are eager to learn by doing.

Soft Skills Matter

There are certain soft skills that apply to any workplace that can also be honed by participating in a school or community play. These talents are different from hard skills, which apply to a specific job—like learning to play an instrument and read music. A few critical soft skills that students can learn in high school theater are:

Oral communication. Everyone in a theater production has to communicate clearly and organize thoughts in an effective way. Every crew member needs to know what has to be done. They often need to give and receive concise instructions. Of course, actors need to feel comfortable speaking in front of an audience— and this certainly translates into other fields. Many employers send their employees to workshops that teach public speaking because it's such an important skill to have. Communication is essential. Being able to stand up in front of a group of people, use your voice with confidence, and effectively communicate a message can help with interviews, business meetings, presentations, and giving speeches. Plus, once you perform in front of a large crowd, you often feel like you can do almost anything.

Problem solving. Mounting a theater production often requires solving problems quickly. A spotlight goes out and a bulb is needed fast. A costume rips and a safety pin proves to be a solution. Keeping confidence and control can go a long way to making things seem fine when things are actually going wrong. Theater people are flexible and ready to change directions if roadblocks arise. Those who learn to improvise may have an even better sense of how to go with the flow, and this can pay off in t he workplace.

Striving for perfection. All theater productions demand perfectionism, and once you get involved in a school or community effort, you'll learn that people involved always want to strive for the absolute best. Theater people are strongly committed to doing things right.

Hard work. Anyone who has thrown himself or herself into a theater production knows what it means to work hard, and this work ethic is appreciated in all sectors of the work world.

Calm in a crisis. If something goes wrong, you learn that it's par for the course, and you look for a solution while keeping a cool exterior. For example, if you're the music director and the microphone dies in the middle of a lead singer's solo, just signal them to keep going and not to show the audience that anything is wrong. This ability can help in almost any job.

Promptness and time management. Theater demands that you show up on time so everyone can rehearse or perform as expected. Showing up on time and doing your job shows dedication as well.

The cast and crew not only know to be on time, but they know how to use what time they have. With a deadline for performance on the horizon, individuals must set a schedule to accomplish all they need to do to have a production up and running on deadline.

Self-discipline. Anyone involved in a show must do some things independently: study the script; learn the music; rehearse scenes with fellow actors; consider the lighting and set design. These activities require you to set aside time for each and stay on track to meet the target date for the performance. Self-discipline is a character trait that all employers want.

Respect for leadership. Although theater people are known for teamwork, they also know that they have to follow the directions of leaders who are guiding the show. People in theater not only know the importance of following a leader, but they know how to assume leadership roles.

Project management. Many businesses need project managers to take a project from A to Z while sticking to a schedule and keeping to a budget. All theater productions demand exactly that. Performing this role in a theater is as good as getting an internship.

Understanding people. Theater brings together diverse people with different personalities. Bringing them together to work toward a common goal is a talent highly valued in the business world. Sometimes, too, business requires dealing with difficult people, and theater provides that experience.

Staging Plays and Selling Homes

Tina Fallon, the producer of the 24-Hour Musicals and 24-Hour Plays, has used her skills in the theater world to launch a successful career selling real estate in Brooklyn. More than twenty years ago, Fallon came up with the fun idea to put on short plays and musicals that were all conceived, written, rehearsed, and presented before a live audience in twenty-four hours. Since then, her concept has grown, and she regularly puts on 24-Hour productions for charity with some of the biggest names in show business, including Naomi Watts, Chris Rock, Julianne Moore, Jennifer Aniston, Edie Falco, Bebe Neuwirth, Tituss Burgess, and Alicia Witt. Her 24-Hour productions have raised millions of dollars for charities. Although she was doing successful work in theater, it still wasn't paying the bills. Some of her friends thought she'd have the talent to be a real estate agent. She had developed confidence and strong leadership skills in theater. She found that working in theater involved coming up with many compromises, and that ability might be well suited the real estate business.

"I love to get people to agree to something, and I don't in any way relish imposing my vision of something on someone else," she said. "Compromising is really an art, and I love to make a deal."

This love of deal making, confidence, and leadership translated from the theater to real estate. Fallon saw the property as the set; the clients, lawyers, and agents were the players; the stagers, movers, and painters were the crew. In the 24-Hour musicals and plays, she's managing the stress of the talent. In real estate, she's managing the stress of the buyers and sellers. Fallon said that she even has an opening, which is the open house, and a final performance, which is the closing. As with producing, she is not in real estate to agree with the buyers' decisions; she is there to be an expert and guide them.

Tina Fallon's theater skills have served her well in a real estate career.

Doing what needs to be done. There is no task beneath anyone in theater. When something needs to be done, you jump in and take action—and that way you may learn many different skills and talents. With a small theater group, an individual has the chance to learn light design, sound engineering, acting, directing, producing, marketing, PR, set design, set construction, ticket sales, budgeting, customer service, ushering, makeup, and costuming. Challenges that come up and require theater troupe members to step out of their comfort zone are often opportunities.

Making do with what you have. Theater people excel at doing quality work with limited means. They often don't have a big budget, so they figure out how to make do with less. Theater people are resourceful.

Joining in a theater production is serious, hard work, but don't forget—it is also great fun.

Thinking seriously about the world. Howard Shalwitz, cofounder of the Woolly Mammoth Theatre Company in Washington, DC, said, "Theater models for us a kind of public discourse that lies at the heart of democratic life and builds our skills for listening to different sides of a conversation or argument and empathizing with the struggles of our fellow human beings whatever their views may be."

A desire to be creative and fun. One characteristic of theater that people might forget is that theater is incredibly fun. The urge to create, be playful, and have some fun can drive any business forward, motivate employees, and help them maintain a sense of dedication and a will to perform their best.

Jobs for the Musically Talented

While skills and traits learned through theater work can translate into different business-world opportunities, those who have training in the music side of theater may want to stick with their passion for music. Beyond live theater, opportunities may be found in television, radio, and film. They also may find opportunities performing and organizing musical shows on cruise ships and at amusement parks, conventions, and fairs. Sometimes, there are niche productions that require music, such as Cirque du Soleil, Disney World, or trade shows. Some with musical talent will continue to work in live theater. Some may even find employment opportunities on Broadway, in major cities, or with regional theater troupes.

Directors. The skills developed as a music director may apply directly to related types of entertainment work. Music directors may work with singers in accompanying their acts in a cabaret format. They may also perform in bands and orchestras. Typically, they understand what it takes to give a good vocal performance, so they can work as vocal and acting coaches as well, giving private lessons to singers and actors.

Often, a music director will teach at a high school or college. A few may try their hand at writing their own music and musicals. They also might find specific jobs calling for musical arrangement (reworking a previously composed piece) or composing some incidental music for plays or advertisements. More and more ad agencies are producing their own digital content, and some may use music. Their musical talents easily transfer over to the worlds of film and television as well. Some find employment in recording studios, working closely with ensembles to get their sounds recorded. Of course, music directors can find work in live theater, too, with employment opportunities on Broadway, in major cities, and with regional theater troupes.

Because they are skilled organizers, directors may transfer their skills to become project managers, entrepreneurs, and business leaders.

Singers/Actors. Singers and actors with singing ability may be hired as background singers who provide backup singing for established artists. They may work on album recordings and in live productions. Singers can find commercial work recording jingles as well. These opportunities require performers who can sing flawlessly with very little rehearsal time. Those who are versatile and can handle different styles of singing will find the most employment. Some singers may have talent to train others, and they can become vocal coaches, teachers, and choir directors. Churches may have positions for professionals who can lead a choir. The world of opera may offer opportunities for singers as well. The singer/actor may also find work in a movie or television show, or providing the voice for a cartoon character or character in a video game. There is also the opportunity to do work in commercials and provide voice-overs. Because singers and actors are outgoing and good at presenting information, they may earn money as salespeople, promoters, and publicists.

Choreographers. Because these professionals design and direct the dance or stylized movement in musical productions, they are very athletic and understand what it takes to be physically fit. They may find their skills transfer to positions as exercise instructors, yoga instructors, and dance teachers.

Musicians. Those who become skilled playing an instrument in theater productions may find that live musicians are needed in recording projects as session musicians and for live concerts by established popular music artists and groups. Films and television shows may also be scored with original music played by orchestras or smaller groups of musicians. Within an orchestra, a musician may find that more skill equals more pay. Principals who play solos are highly valued. Dance groups often need trained musicians, whether they are presenting a performance, rehearsing, or teaching dance moves to others. Musicians also find work teaching in

Those who have honed their talents on stage may find opportunities to teach others.

schools, colleges, and universities, or giving private lessons. Some go on to write or arrange music and may end up providing the score for television shows, movies, or computer games. Because they often have a keen knowledge of musical instruments, they can find work in music retail stores selling or repairing instruments. (Many top guitar players have worked at Guitar Center, the largest chain of musical instrument retailers in the world.) There can be very specific niche work as well—for example, developing ring tones for cell phones.

Sound designer. The sound designer plans and provides the sound effects in the play or musical; he or she also may be in charge of music from existing sources. Many double as the sound engineer, who runs the actual sounds and assures all equipment is functioning correctly. With these skills, one may find a career as a recording engineer in a studio. They typically need specific educational training to develop the skills to record professionally. They not only operate the equipment to record, they understand how to mix the sounds and produce a final product that may be used in making a commercial album for a musical artist, a commercial, or music for a video game, film, radio production, or television show. Because recording engineers work closely with musicians and vocalists, it can be helpful to have proficiency in a musical instrument or singing.

Those who operate the sounds and control microphone levels during the show are called sound board operators, and they may use their talents to help present rock concerts and other live arena performances. For instance, sound board operators are needed by many businesses that give live presentations to their employees, or venues such as aquariums, planetariums, and sporting events may have live show segments that require a professional to assure that the audio is being properly controlled so an audience can hear it. Sports arenas use sound people to enhance the game experience. Through working on the audio side in theater productions, a person may develop a specific talent for creating sound effects—these services may also be needed in the world of video game, film, and TV production. Because they have an appreciation for music and the ability to set up audio equipment, a sound designer or sound board operator may transfer those abilities into work as a DJ, playing prerecorded music at parties, weddings, and other celebrations.

So no matter what your interests are, joining in a theater production is worth it on many levels, from developing workplace skills to making personal connections that can lead to strong friendships or career connections. Above all, theater is fun and exciting, and the experience is unforgettable. As the great director Alfred Hitchcock said, "What is drama but life with the dull bits cut out."

Sound editors can find many markets that can use their computer skills.

GLOSSARY

apron In a traditional theater, the part of the stage that projects in front of the curtain.

bar A segment of time in music corresponding to a set number of beats.

barn door An attachment of four metal panels on a theatrical light to control the light beam.

batten A long metal pipe suspended above the stage, from which lighting, theatrical scenery, and stage curtains are hung.

beginners Cast members who are on the stage as the curtain rises.

blocking The exact staging or positioning of the actors in a play.

book The script of the play or the libretto of a musical.

corpse To laugh or cause an actor to laugh unexpectedly on stage.

cue An instruction given by a stage manager, such as "Cue the red spotlight." It is also a signal for someone to perform a function, such as when to come onstage.

curtain call When the cast takes a bow at the end of the show.

diaphragm A large muscle sheath that stretches across the bottom of the rib cage. Using the muscle properly can aid a singing performance and reduce stress on the vocal cords.

dips Electrical sockets set into the stage floor or the floors in the wings.

downstage The area on the stage toward the audience.

dresser A person who helps cast members make quick costume changes.

embouchure The shape the lips must take on the mouthpiece of a brass or woodwind instrument to play it correctly.

footlights Flood lights placed on the stage floor at the front of a stage.

harmony Two or more musical notes played at the same time, usually to produce a pleasing sound.

legs Curtains used to cover the wings.

off book Rehearsing from memory instead of reading from a script.

on book Rehearsing while holding a script, done before actors have had time to memorize their parts.

preproduction All the steps and work needed to be completed before the opening night of a theater piece.

prompt corner The place from which the stage manager controls the show.

props Short for "properties," the small items that actors may use in the action onstage or simply add to the stage set.

rehearsal call An instruction to attend rehearsal.

rig To set the lighting in position.

set dressing The items on a set, such as books in a bookshelf.

sightlines The area of the stage that can be seen by everyone in the audience.

stage left On the left side of a stage from the point of view of a performer facing the audience.

strike To dismantle the set.

triad A set of three notes, usually in thirds, that creates a type of harmony.

trills Rapid alternations between two adjacent notes.

understudy An actor who learns the part of a leading actor and is rehearsed and ready to step into the role if that actor is unable to perform.

upstage At the back of the stage, or when one actor deliberately draws attention to him or herself at the expense of another.

vamp A repeating musical figure that is played until the next actor comes on stage or completes a motion.

wings The sides of the stage out of sight from the audience where actors wait to make their entrances.

FOR MORE INFORMATION

Books

Belli, Mary Lou, and Dinah Lenney. *Acting for Young Actors: The Ultimate Teen Guide*. New York: Back Stage Books, 2006.

Boal, Augusto. *Games for Actors and Non-Actors*. New York: Routlege, 2002.

Ceraso, Chris, and Michael Bernard. *The Teen Acting Ensemble: A Practical Guide to Doing Theater with Teenagers*. New York: Dramatist Play Service, Inc., 2002.

Gerle, Andrew. *The Enraged Accompanist's Guide to the Perfect Audition*. Milwaukee, WI: Applause Theatre & Cinema Books, 2011.

Lerch, Louise. *Broadway for Teens (Songbook): Young Women's Edition*. Milwaukee, WI: Hal Leonard, 2005.

Schumacher, Thomas, and Jeff Kurtti. *How Does the Show Go On: An Introduction to the Theater*. New York: Disney Editions, 2007.

Websites

Educational Theatre Association
https://www.schooltheatre.org/home
News, festival schedules, tutorials, links (including one for jobs), and blog posts on teaching theater can be found on this comprehensive site.

Musical101.com:
http://www.musicals101.com
Billed as a cyber encyclopedia of musical theatre, film, and television, this site contains links to biographies, histories, instructional stories, and anything else you may want to know about show business.

SFKids
http://www.sfskids.org/conduct
This site shows some of the fundamentals of conducting an orchestra.

Videos

Berinstein, Dori. *Show Business: The Road to Broadway.* Dramatic Forces, 2007.

Donnelly, Laurie (executive producer). *Broadway or Bust.* Boston: PBS/WGBH, 2012.

Kallis, Matthew. *Most Valuable Players.* Beverly Hills, CA: Canyonback Films, 2010.

INDEX

Page numbers in **boldface** are illustrations. Entries in **boldface** are glossary terms.

ABOUT THE AUTHOR

Don Rauf has written more than thirty nonfiction books, mostly for young adults. Titles include *Actor* (Virtual Apprentice series), *Recording Industry* (Career Launcher series), *The Rise and Fall of the Ottoman Empire*, *Simple Rules for Card Games*, *and Killer Lipstick and Other Spy Gadgets.* Don writes and performs music with the New York City band Life in a Blender. He currently lives in Seattle with his wife, Monique, and son, Leo.